That Dog Just Don't Hunt

Create a powerful and purposeful workforce
by selecting and keeping the right employees

by
Charles N. Acker

Bloomington, IN  Milton Keynes, UK

authorHOUSE®

AuthorHouse™
1663 Liberty Drive, Suite 200
Bloomington, IN 47403
www.authorhouse.com
Phone: 1-800-839-8640

AuthorHouse™ UK Ltd.
500 Avebury Boulevard
Central Milton Keynes, MK9 2BE
www.authorhouse.co.uk
Phone: 08001974150

First published by AuthorHouse 2/27/2007

ISBN: 978-1-4259-7115-1 (sc)

Printed in the United States of America
Bloomington, Indiana

This book is printed on acid-free paper.

Library of Congress Control Number: 2006911253

Table of Contents

Introduction

That Dog Just Don't Hunt has nothing to do with hunting in the traditional sense. It does, however, offer to guide us into a new way of discovering answers to apparent employee/business deficiencies. The issues that we will uncover are fundamental to developing a healthy and thriving workplace. This treatise will obviously not address every workplace issue. However, it will offer sound, tried-and-true principles that can be used in many, many situations. Some managers will scoff at the simplicity offered herein and others will ponder their techniques and sharpen their skills. Finally, some managers that have a good working relationship with their employees will feel validated—as they should. Regardless of your skill level, as in hunting, we must be clear on our targets, explore new landscape, work tirelessly, and be keen to signs that will lead us to success.

As an executive, I've heard countless managers declare, unashamedly, that a particular employee isn't making the kind of progress in a job that was expected when they were interviewed and ultimately hired. In other related cases, tenured employees may seem content to produce lackluster work or complain incessantly about how the company is being managed. They don't appear to care anymore or to have "a fire in their belly." Tragically, both of these cases often lead to profit declines and cost overruns. The employee is either terminated or passed over for advancement because of our perception of their performance. I say *tragically* because in many cases the problem isn't the fault of the employee. It's the fault of management—employees suffer for management's failures. The outcome of this tragedy is that our business is stuck in a rut and we're hard-pressed to turn it back into a thriving enterprise with purpose and vision. Believing that our *employees* are the sole problem of our business deficiencies leads me to reply, "That dog just don't hunt!"

Let's face the facts, there are *many* reasons employees don't reach the level of performance that we expect of them. We all have our reasons and varied experiences on that score. Some managers have many employees and some have few employees—regardless of the number—management must resolve the problems in the workplace to have a productive environment. Akin to hunting, there are many signs, but to follow the right one to success is often difficult—so to begin our quest, we need to look IN, not out!

Looking IN requires an honest evaluation of ME. Creating a purposful workforce starts with a clear, measurable roadmap on how we intend to run our business, to identify our purpose, to get where we want to go, to bag the game. Sharing your purpose with employees doesn't always energize them to adopt it as their own. Rather, we must identify *employee* goals and blend those together to build a powerful workforce dedicated to targeted objectives. This isn't to say that everyone will have the same purpose in the workforce, but they all should share foundational elements of the objectives used to achieve *the* purpose. In the interest of delving into obstacles to success, we must go "hunting" to discover insights into diverse purposes and how we can direct them to our business advantage.

To create a powerful, purposeful workforce, we must consider alternate trails, together with pitfalls and crests.

Through years of practical experience, painful decisions, and soul-searching discussions with fellow managers, I'll share with you the root causes that I've found for employee performance issues. My hope is that by investigating these causes we can help our employees, and ultimately our businesses, succeed, and we can understand and adapt a *manager/employee growth relationship* that supports our purpose. Furthermore, this *growth relationship* identifies the techniques that good managers should be using to assist with the development of subordinates. Isn't that what a *good* manager should do? If you have a boss, isn't that philosophy what you'd hope he or she would adopt when considering your performance? If you are the boss, you will undoubtedly consider some of these principles as potential setbacks for the profitability of your business. Remember, however, that anything of value requires an investment. Much of this book deals with a time investment, not a cash outlay. Additionally, we'll challenge some accepted corporate ideals, such as: Can real, <u>positive</u> changes be influenced through an "annual employee performance appraisal" process? Does a pay raise spur employee loyalty and performance? Is the newest generation simply not cut out to recognize that business is there to make a reasonable profit?

Remember, the growth relationship provides that as employees grow, so does the business, but corporate growth doesn't necessarily equal employee growth. There's a balance between these two components that must be equal. The company has to continue *growing* its human resource as it grows itself. Otherwise, the sustainability of corporate growth will fail because the employees do not keep up with the growth trend, resulting in turnover and dissatisfaction among the ranks.

The more your business grows, the more you need to heed the lessons offered herein. The ideal development is to create a *learning* culture so the skills of your workers keep pace with the complexities that a growing business presents. As you read through this collection of ideas, and if you find that *you're* an employee who is facing a question about your ability, loyalty, or performance in the workplace, give your boss a copy of this book. It just might make a difference—that's what it was written for.

I recognize that concepts like those found in books like this one are often difficult to manufacture into meaningful and productive techniques that the reader can apply in their particular situation. With that in mind, I will provide anecdotes and specific examples, as well as creative templates so you'll come away with more than just my ideas. Additionally, I'll offer clues throughout the book in an attempt to clarify the points I'm trying to make. One will be a "great idea"—you're on the right track—and suggest a singular reference to positive insights, while obviously refers to management techniques that, although common, may contradict the ideals of employee development that will promote soaring performance.

I hope that you'll enjoy this book and that it will provide some thought-provoking ideas that will enhance the enjoyment of your workplace and the effectiveness of your relationship with your employees—to the end that a powerful, purposeful workforce can thrive within your organization. For my fellow managers, *That Dog Just Don't Hunt* explores target areas common to employees who fail to perform to our satisfaction—good management means continually searching for improvement, so *let's go hunting*.

Topical outline:

The origin of That Dog Just Don't Hunt...

I developed the initial outline for what was to become a successful lecture series and finally this composition while on a flight to Fairbanks, Alaska, where my boss had dispatched me to terminate a mid-level manager.

His last words to me as I left the office that day were, *"Why didn't Jim perform the job the way we expected him to?"*

Many other managers faced with that question may have simply shrugged their shoulders. Well, I didn't. The question lingered in my mind like an aromatic fragrance leaves its imprint on our senses. I was so bothered by the question that I spent the next four hours, cramped into my bulkhead seat on the airplane, scribbling ideas that were later boiled down to form the **Big Five** (a sixth point was added later, but is actually reserved for managers.)

I began applying these ideas immediately upon my arrival in Fairbanks, and I continue to use them successfully to this day. While I can't claim 100 percent employee improvement, I feel quite satisfied that the workplace and the relationship that I have with my employees has improved dramatically. I have a much better understanding of the issues that impede business success and I can recognize and remove barriers that cause disatisfaction and costly employee turnover. I must admit, these principles have likely been offered by other writers with better descriptive powers than I, but I believe the real power of these ideals rests in their simplicity.

A lesson from the dog dish...

A truism that I learned about the workplace was inadvertantly developed on my back patio, and I owe credit to Duke, my chocolate Laborador, for its value. I purchased a home in Louisiana on the lake. The home was nice. It had a pool and boathouse. I soon determined that new lawn furniture for the patio was in order. (The patio was Duke's home. He was an "outdoor" dog and good hunter.) Soon after placing my furniture in a nice pattern near the pool, I began noticing bird droppings on the chairs. Since the patio was covered, I couldn't figure out how the birds had come to stain my new furniture. Duke was a *bird dog*. He'd surely keep birds away, wouldn't he?

One day, I noticed a bird sitting on the back of one of the chairs. I started to chase it off, but stopped and waited to see what would happen. Duke was lounging on the patio, his big belly outstretched to the sun. He had one eye on the bird that, although wary, seemed content to stay put—why, I wondered? Duke closed his eyes and the bird obviously recognized an opportunity and swooped into the open bowl, leaving with a beakful of dry dog food.

I was amazed at the little bird's courage to challenge a big, burly dog. I imagined Duke springing into action to chase off the tiny thief, but Duke just lay there, content to enjoy his nap. I couldn't believe it! *The birds were eating all of his food, and he didn't seem concerned about it in the slightest*!

"What kind of bird dog are you?" I questioned, but he just squinted his eyes against the sun and flopped out a large pink tongue as he panted his reply with that constant "smile" for which Labs are known.

I quickly reasoned that he was **conditioned by me** and knew that even if the birds took all of his food, I'd simply fill his bowl up for him when he was hungry. He felt no need to protect it. I was the provider! Immediately, I recognized a pattern, one I'd seen with my employees—they were satisfied to wait for me to keep their bowl full while the competition stole our food. Why should my employees care? No need to worry. Their bowl would be filled again, wouldn't it? Hadn't I always provided for them? I had conditioned them to be careless.

I learned a powerful lesson from the dog dish on that sunny afternoon, and it had all started with bird poop! What could I do to encourage our employees to be vigilant about our resources and our customers? To help reduce waste and to keep our "patio furniture" clean? To consistently deliver the service that our customers expected?

Why didn't many of them seem to care? The answer was simple. I didn't *make* them care. When they needed a new computer, I bought one. If a tool was missing in the shop, I bought a new one. If someone felt overworked, I hired more staff. If a vehicle was damaged, I had it fixed. I accepted all ownership and required none from them. Oh, I thought I was doing things right, providing the resources my staff needed, but after that lesson, I looked with renewed interest at what was happening at the workplace. My employees were complacent. They had become lazy and cared little about doing their share to keep costs in check and customers coming back. The puzzle I faced was: what to do about it? But now, back to the hunt at hand.

The days of enlightenment...

The flight I took to Fairbanks from Seattle was packed with tourists off to explore the interior of Alaska before the first big snows would make traveling the state treacherous. I sat in a bulkhead seat next to the window. The words of my boss wove their way through my mind, like grapevines clinging around a fencepost. I knew Jim, the target of my mission, and considered him a friend. This was going to be difficult at best. He knew I was coming, but he had no idea how it would impact him.

The interesting thing was that Jim was in a management role himself. He was considered a mid-level manager, with front line supervisory responsibility. It was his job to ensure that those employees dealing directly with our customers were doing the job correctly. Nonetheless, of all the corporate communications he had been involved in, none of them had tipped him off to management's disenchantment with him. The company kept its opinions about his performance deeply hidden from view—even worse, from Jim himself.

Residing in a mid-level management position may be one of the most tenuous places to be in an organization, caught between decision-makers and "payroll takers."

 **Failing to ensure that our employees are aware of how we believe they're performing leads to failure.**

I caught my flight at Sea-Tac, just south of Seattle, and hunkered down in my seat for the long ride. It was a smooth takeoff, and the service was timely and pleasant. Meal service came soon after leveling off at 31,000 feet. As I worked my way through the meal, I closely watched the flight attendant perform her duties. She was *efficiency in motion*, and went about her business with a smile. She clearly appeared to enjoy her job—not a common attribute within the service industry these days. Within an hour, the attendant noticed that I had finished my dinner and my meal tray was quickly removed (that was a time when airlines provided more than pretzels). I pulled out a large legal pad and began to write down my thoughts by the light of the mis-aimed reading lamp. My choppy writing depicted the jagged flight, tossed effortlessly by the turbulence of the air perched above the cold mountains of Alaska.

Deep in thought, I was interrupted… "Coffee?"

The attendant beckoned, her words dripping like honey from smiling lips painted cherry red. I looked up and was immediately disarmed by her features.

"No, thanks," I muttered. But then I thought again, coffee just might be refreshing after all, "Sure, why not?"

I quickly reversed my answer—too late—since she was already on to the next passenger. I watched the attendant move, her smile never wavering, even though the responses to her offer were mixed at best.

At that moment, **BIG 1** flushed like a pair of feisty pheasants from tall grass!

1.

Natural Ability

The foundation of a powerful workforce

With a certain amount of shock, I suddenly realized that what I was observing in that flight attendant was exactly the personality and mannerisms that I presumed were required for her job. She had a quality about her that defined courtesy, job enjoyment, and grace. It appeared to me that her delight in service was genuine, not manufactured. That forte wasn't an aspect of her job that could be drilled into her, at least not if it would be consistent on every flight. I certainly embrace the notion that training *can* make an impact on employee behavior, although I further believe it's usually for dedicated tasks. It takes natural talent to **want** do the job right every single day.

Take, for example, a car salesman who is an introvert by nature. How many cars do you think that person might sell? How about a ballplayer who doesn't possess the timing to catch a ball in flight or an accountant who struggles with math? I'm sure you get my point: *align natural talents to the right job task within your organization.* Play to the strengths of your staff, not to their weaknesses—a blending of purpose. How does one know their strengths? There are three fundamental tools I have learned to use over the years:

1. Communicate with employees to expound on the objective and to get their endorsement of it, because without their buy-in, no objective is worth its salt.

2. Draft a position analysis with objectives for what you need accomplished.

3. Measure performance against determined objectives.

1. Communication:

I'm not referring to idle chitchat in the workplace nor am I referring to using emails to give direction! Communication involves a two-way discussion of issues important to your objectives. Target your discussion to identify those qualities that you're looking for. Ask them what they feel is the most personally rewarding part of their job. Your charge as a manager is to continuously develop or identify capabilities among your staff that will enhance corporate growth and stability—directed energy toward the purpose. In essence, what you're doing is creating a *culture* that will support your overall business objectives. As in hunting, know your target from all angles. Keep the tasks concise!

For example, I had a manager working for me who had a *global* position, meaning that he had to complete ALL diverse tasks and priorities. That meant accounting, training, supervising subordinates, reading reports, financial analysis, selling, and recruiting. His best talent was writing, but he felt bogged down in all of the other aspects of his job. His performance wasn't the best it could be because he didn't possess the natural talents necessary to perform the functions at his highest potential.

I'm NOT suggesting that we hire specialists for each and every task that's to be performed by a worker. Rather, through communication, find the areas they excel in and see if you can assign them more of that, which will breed job satisfaction because the employee will feel good about doing good work! Employee *staying power* means that their reward is in seeing the purpose advanced—not in pleasing you.

In the case of my worker with a talent for writing, I took a little bit of that particular requirement away from other workers who were struggling with it and gave the first worker more of what he was good at. This had a twofold positive impact on my department's effectiveness:

1. He performed that task in less time and much more succinctly than his co-workers.

2. It reduced the stress of the others who had difficulty with it, allowing them to concentrate on the tasks *they* did well.

From that lesson, I learned quickly how to blend workers to tasks, and it has had a positive impact on the mood of the group as a whole. As a department, we achieved more work product than we did before I learned that valuable rule. While that lesson occurred before the concept of the Big Six was developed, I recognized it as an application of *natural ability.* As a side note, that lesson wouldn't have been learned had I not been hunting and communicating in search of improvement.

Let's quickly review some *time-honored* theories about communication.

- ✓ Communication should always be a two-way event.
- ✓ Seek feedback from the other party to ensure clarity.
- ✓ Communicate often.
- ✓ Keep work-related communications professional.
- ✓ Make certain that communications aren't threatening.
- ✓ Seek a neutral location for sensitive communications.
- ✓ Follow up to be sure that your direction is heeded.
- ✓ Communicate in a manner that suits the issue.
- ✓ Learn as many facts as possible.

How does one communicate to discover natural talent? That type of conversation should be aimed at more personal interests, though not too personal mind you. For example, when I interview a candidate or converse with a tenured employee, I want to know who their heroes are. That does two things: it disarms them and makes them feel comfortable and allows them to talk about themselves. (I've known few people that didn't enjoy talking about themselves.) Determining a hero who influenced an employee's behavior or objectives often leads me to crucial information about that employee as a person.

For example, if an employee responds that Mickey Mantle is a hero to them, seek more. You may find out that they enjoy team sports. That person will likely understand team concepts. It's also a clue to the employee's aspirations and where you have aspirations, it's not too far a leap to find some *natural talent*. After all, birds of a feather flock together.

When discussing heroes, I often hear that a parent is their chief idol. The reasons are many, but it usually involves a personal sacrifice of some kind. That may indicate a solid work ethic. Once an employee clearly defines who their heroes are and why, determine how that information fits within *your* purpose. Developing a powerful team begins by creating a common objective. The real test for you in finding the right employee is based on your ability to accurately gauge their *will* to work in your organization. If there is *will*, performance will be easier to develop.

I'll sum up communication by offering our old friend Daniel Webster's definition: *"Communication: 4. To be connected, as rooms."*

Think about that for a moment. The word *Rooms* indicates a separate, yet connected, unit among several. Each <u>room</u> may have a unique and distinct purpose within the whole. If you think about it, that meaning is very much like common corporate departments—a group made up of distinct employees with unique purposeful contributions to our objectives. *Communication* actually refers to the connection between rooms – a passageway, a means of tying them together. Interpersonal rapport.

Sometimes we're our own worst enemy. If we don't take the time to recruit, interview, and hire the correct *room,* we deserve whatever we get. That's easy for me to say, isn't it? Perhaps you don't have the luxury of hiring your staff. Maybe in your organization that task is left up to the dreaded Human Resources Department. No matter whether you do the hiring or not, you still have the obligation to your company to provide accurate feedback to the HR Department so they can hire the right person. Let's not kid ourselves. An HR manager can only hire the right employee for you if they're fully aware of the requirements of a position. Nonetheless, in any organization, the supervising manager should have the final approval of any candidate in their charge.

Hiring the **right employee** with the **natural capacity** for a task is tough. Begin your search inside your organization – it may be easier to transfer an employee from a foundational position rather to locate a replacement, especially for specialized skill sets. Tough you bet, but there are many resources available to help you make a selection. For example, there are numerous firms that use a series of tests to measure aptitude and ability. Many of these assessments are relatively inexpensive when you consider the negative implications and ultimate heartache of hiring *wrong.* Consider seeking outside help if needed.

2. Position Analysis

Before we can ever get to the hiring stage, we must first know the tasks that are to be performed. That's where the *position analysis* that I referred to earlier comes into play. You must detail each aspect of the job—and keep it fundamental and to the point. Let's do a position analysis for a flight attendant together to see how one works. For the sake of this book, we may make up some tasks, since we may not be totally familiar with what a flight attendant does. When you see it, however, you may find out that you can do an analysis whether you know the job well or not. (Note: It differs from a *job description*. Whereas a job description lists the duties, a position analysis clearly defines the precise steps that are necessary to perform the duties.)

BASIC POSITION ANALYSIS - FLIGHT ATTENDANT

Task	Duration	Skills or Knowledge required
Standing	Constant	Balance
Food service	Two hours	Food service training Health and safety training
Safety instruction	15 min.	Safety training, public speaking intercom use, demonstration
Customer service	Constant	Positive demeanor, excellent communication skills, knowledge of flight schedules, problem resolution, systems knowledge
Emergency procedures	Spontaneous	Emergency training, self-control, excellent communication skills
Bending, lifting	Occasionally	Able to lift 40 lbs overhead

You see that I keep the analysis quite simple and touch only on the fundamental aspects of the job. Obviously, this form could be as detailed as necessary. For example, under *Food service*, one could list all of the tasks associated with that function: oven use, opening bottles or cans, loading and unloading carts, pushing and locking carts, storage of utensils and carts, etc. Normally, however, those aspects of the job can be trained and natural talent isn't a qualifying point. On the other hand, positive demeanor, excellent communication skills, knowledge of systems (implying reading and retention of information), and able to lift forty pounds are attributes that an applicant should bring to the job.

What can you think of that a flight attendant needs as natural qualities to perform the tasks associated with that profession? I'm certain that you noticed *standing* as a qualification and may have scratched your head, wondering why something so obvious would be listed. I also noted *balance* as a prerequisite for the task. A flight attendant must have balance to walk up and down a moving, jolting airplane. That type of entry would likely be used on a safety-related task analysis. (A task analysis is a breakdown of the tasks in minute detail—unlike a position analysis, which categorizes fundamental aspects of the job.) Some of the others that may be included in such a safety-related overview could be: bending, crouching, lifting, hand strength, hearing, and so on. Your position analysis would also list the percentage of time each of those aspects is used as an average on a particular flight. (Don't forget the American's with Disabilities Act! Depending upon the task that you require, special assistance may be required for employees who may have a qualifying disability.) The employee MUST know the requirements and performance objectives of the job. The **performance analysis** can really help you choose candidates that can fit into your organization and handle the requirements of the tasks at hand. In the case of the flight attendant, she made my purchase more enjoyable and comfortable. Will I fly that airline again? Absolutely! What does all this have to do with you as a manager, ensuring that your employees can perform to *your* expectations? Simply this: If you have high expectations for their job performance, you'll ensure that they meet them and you'll select the right applicants to work in your company.

A common complaint from employees that aren't performing well is that they haven't been trained. That's often a cop-out. They've been trained, but for some reason, they just can't perform the task to your expectations. By developing tests or quizzes for tasks, you can always pull out the employee's test scores to see if they passed a question or failed it. For example, with a flight attendant, we may have a task of rinsing, drying, and stacking trays in a transfer cart for vendor pickup at the end of the flight. If an employee isn't rinsing, drying, or stacking them correctly and, when challenged on their performance, insists that they weren't trained correctly, check their test. If you develop a test to accompany the training you provide, one multiple-choice question may be as follows:

1. When preparing dinner trays for transfer at the end of the flight, you must:

(Choose *best* answer.)

A. Stack and secure trays in transfer cart.

B. Rinse, dry, and stack trays in transfer cart.

C. Leave trays on meal carts for vendor transfer.

Such quizzes aren't designed to test memory, rather performance and validation of training. The next time an employee challenges a performance deficiency by adopting the "nobody trained me" excuse; simply pull out their test to verify the complaint. If they failed a question, then you have to evaluate your training program. However, if they gave the correct answer on the test, it was just an excuse for poor performance. Regardless, the employee's job performance can be judged fairly and improved by using tests.

Measuring an employee's skills is kind of tricky in today's litigious world. Finding people who have both the aptitude and desire to work in your business is the key to successful recruiting. Not everyone you interview will have both attributes, so your questions must be directed to the element you feel most needed. Aptitude can be achieved through task repetition, but only when the task is being performed correctly. Desire can be achieved through incentives. Fundamental capacity is a learned behavior.

This brings up a good rule to follow: *Be certain to communicate your expectations to your employees.* Remember the first danger sign I noted: *Failing to keep our employees aware of how they're performing.* If they understand what your expectations are, it makes adjusting that performance a much easier chore for you. Employees generally assume that if they don't hear from you, they're performing to your expectations. WRONG! Tip: *Unacceptable behavior that goes uncorrected becomes acceptable behavior.* Correcting that behavior too late is like waiting until you're completely out of clean underwear to do the laundry! Communication must be continual and to the point. That means when you look in the *sock drawer*, pay attention!

For example, young people who are available once school is out for the season fill many service jobs. A real problem to that "fit" is that those service workers may not know what *service* means if we consider that many conveniences are now **self-serve**. Younger workers simply haven't had an example to build the aptitude. There is self-serve gas, self-serve banking, self-serve groceries, self-serve tickets for the movies, and the list goes on. Even the food we eat is prepared in advance so we can just pop it in the microwave. What level of service experience do you think this generation has developed? To expect them to perform at the same service level that previous generations experienced is foreign, unrealistic, and obscure. Remember when a gas station attendant would actually check your oil and wash your windshield? When has any of the newest generation of service workers observed that level of attention? Those young service workers simply haven't experienced it. Therefore, it must be exemplified for them. Have you heard the catchall phrase that our *internal* customers are as important as our *external* customers? How may times do you greet your employees with enthusiasm, treat them with care, and let them know how important they are to you? Exemplify your expected service level to external customers by exploring it with your internal customers on a day-to-day basis.

OK, you have your position analysis and you're getting some ideas about measuring their aptitude, but you still don't know where to find potential candidates. That brings up a crucial point that's often missed by many companies: *advertising* for a job isn't *recruiting*—it's simply ADVERTISING!

I can't begin to tell you how many times I've heard the statement, "We put an ad in the paper, but we can't get anyone to apply!" That's because they failed to understand what recruiting is all about. Any good coach knows how to recruit: *go to the places where potential players are performing, observe their talent, and then tantalize them into coming to play for your team.*

Let's see what our old friend Mr. Webster has to say about *recruiting*, shall we? Open your dictionary and you'll see, *"To enlist new members."* Well, that's not particularly helpful, is it? Let's look up *enlist*: *"To secure for a cause."* Now that's better. What's the *cause* for the job you're recruiting for? Accounting? Secretary? Bus Driver? What's the *cause* for that function within your organization? I'm not referring to the *reason* for the position, since that's self-explanatory, but rather for the ideals of the job or task. *"Cause: An ideal or goal to which a person is dedicated."* Whew! Now we're getting closer. Old Danny doesn't make this easy on us, does he?

One more now; *"Goal: The result toward which effort is directed."* WOW! Check out *"Advertise: To describe or announce publicly."* Do you see that advertising and recruiting are different? Announcing an open position doesn't guarantee that you'll attract the kind of people you need. If you use advertising to enlist applicants, then outlining the job duties in the advertisement helps to limit candidates to those who can perform the tasks. Advertising **does** work, however, because it increases the number of potential candidates to choose from. However, if you *recruit* after observing a candidate in action, it will reduce the time necessary to make a selection from a multitude of candidates, and it also increases the chance for a successful fit within your organization.

> People who are good at what they do are generally already employed and don't necessarily take the time to read the want ads. That means *you must* find them.

An analogy from my first goose hunt...

To illustrate the difference between advertising and recruiting, I'll share the lessons I learned from my first goose hunt. Growing up in the Norman Rockwell generation (*the* artist whose work depicted the simple everyday events of life) I wanted to experience the thrill of bringing home a Christmas goose for our holiday supper. I had visions of a roasted goose, browned from the oven and stuffed with cranberries, raisins, herbs, and bread.

I planned my trip to eastern Washington in early December. The air was cold and crisp and the golden leaves of fall had long since drifted to earth on the cool winds of November. Bare tree branches stretched out across the horizon appearing as cracks in the deep blue winter sky.

I selected a small pond near a known *flyway* (migratory birds follow common pathways as they head south for the winter and back north for the summer months) and placed my decoys in a welcoming pattern on the frigid waters. I hunkered down in my *blind* (a brushy area on the shoreline used for concealment, since ducks and geese have uncanny eyesight and can decipher threats easily from the air) and awaited my trophy. I sipped hot coffee from my thermos and watched Duke as he scanned the skies with alert golden eyes.

I'd been crouched for just over an hour when I noticed Duke's ears perk up and his gaze lock on something in the distance. I soon heard the distinct call of geese in formation and I pinpointed a small V of black dots low on the horizon. Geese, and they were headed right for my pond! I quickly checked my twelve-gauge shotgun and slipped my trigger finger out of my warm shooting glove. I felt the icy cold air grip my bare neck and the sheer excitement caused me to shudder.

As the **V** grew closer, I could see that the geese had set their wings to come in for a landing near my decoys. I waited and watched them gracefully glide closer and closer. Duke shivered and his teeth chattered with anticipation. As the V drew closer, I counted thirteen Canadian honkers. I needed to be patient, to allow them to come into the decoys so I could get a quick kill with my #2 shells. They swooped and glided and circled to land, but at the last second, decided that something wasn't quite right. Had they seen me lying in wait? What had spooked them when they'd seemed so ready to drop into the decoys?

Nevertheless, they were close enough for a kill as they glided across the pond in front of me. I had to shoot NOW! I rose up and as the thrill gripped me, I shot, once, twice, three times. The smoke drifted away as I watched the geese fly off into the distant horizon, not one of them hit by my shots! I looked at the geese and then looked at Duke. Disappointedly, he peered at the geese, then at the pond, and then back up at me. I looked at my gun, I looked at the geese, and then I sat down dejectedly. Duke whined and I patted his head. What happened I asked myself? The geese had easily been in range and they certainly had made large enough targets, gliding effortlessly over the decoys.

It took me a few seconds, but then I realized what had happened. I had fired at the *flock* and not at a specific bird. I knew that I missed every one of them cleanly, since there wasn't a feather floating anywhere in sight.

The final two days of the hunt were truly enjoyable as I decided to explore the area with Duke rather than to try again. I figured that I'd had my chance—and that a turkey from the local supermarket would be just as tasty.

The great lesson of that story is to focus and pick a target. Don't mistakenly take a shotgun approach to advertising for candidates! For example, let's look at two different ads:

HELP WANTED	**The Electric Coffee Bean**
New coffee shop seeks service workers. Must be personable. Excellent wages and benefits. Please call 555-5555 to apply.	A new midtown coffee shop is looking for team members. Must be 18 years or older. Excellent wages and benefits. Call 555-5555 for a complete job description.

Obvious, isn't it? The one on the right tells the candidate the name of the business and where it's located—in *midtown*. Depending upon where a candidate lives, they may not want to drive or work in midtown, thereby limiting the scope of the applicant pool. Additionally, a candidate must meet an age limitation and be willing to work in a team environment. Furthermore, they can get a complete description by calling the listed number. That's an important point. While the first ad tells candidates how to apply for a job, the second ad indicates additional steps to take should they be interested. By providing a description of requirements, candidates will eliminate themselves should the job not be for them. That will save *you* time and trouble.

As you can see, the ads are close, but distinct, and the one on the right is much more focused. What you're looking for are *candidates* not *applicants.* Your objective is *to develop a pool of possible candidates* so you may focus your recruiting effort! Bear in mind that the above example is oversimplified. If you don't have the resources to have a professional draft your ad, at least take time to review other ads in your newspaper to find examples of those that pique your interest. That's also an excellent way to see what's happening with your competition!

The rules of recruiting dictate that employees want to feel wanted. Showing your interest in them tantalizes *their* interest in working for you. I use my business card. I printed a little note on the back that says I'd like to talk to them about working for me. It gives my phone number and the company I work for on the reverse. I can't begin to tell you how effective that inexpensive little tool is. I almost always get a call from them. Why? Because I showed *my* interest. Recruit in your everyday life, at the drugstore, the dry cleaner, or the restaurant. They're places where you can observe potential employees performing their functions. As the coach, go find *them* performing their tasks to see if they have the abilities you're looking for.

By now, you may be asking the obvious question: where does *natural talent* come from? I remember reading an article in the *Seattle Times* newspaper some time ago, titled "Scientists locate brain's own egg timer." The article declared that scientists had located the part of the brain that measures time and distance, much like our circadian clock keeps us on time. The article went on to say that those scientists didn't know how they'd apply their discovery, but it was important.

"Hmm," I said to myself. "It seems that they've uncovered the methods a driver uses to interact with other traffic, kind of like geese keeping a formation in flight."

Traffic interaction is all about time, distance, and computing the variances in other vehicle's speed and location. Therefore, if you're looking for a professional safe driver, you should measure each candidate's *brain egg timer* by testing concentration during stressful scenes to select a driver with the ability to focus their concentration while balancing a multitude of diverse stimuli.

Natural talent is often first discovered in preschool activities. I call it *intrinsic interest*. Kids gravitate to what they're interested in, and what they're interested in often determines their developing the necessary skills to perform that activity.

Natural talent can also be replaced by *developed experience.* Train, train, train, and give your employees opportunities outside their current roles! You may be surprised to find new ideas, innovations and creative solutions to tired old problems.

I'll use yet another hunting analogy to refine my point. The ideas in this composition suggest that we wouldn't take a French poodle duck hunting and expect positive results. The poodle has many fine qualities, but retrieving ducks from cold water isn't one of them.

In Richard Wolter's acclaimed training manual, *Water Dog*, we learn that Labrador retrievers were selected by duck hunters because of their capacity to withstand cold water and severe conditions—and their natural affinity to *retrieve.* As Wolter teaches, even though the Lab has such natural talents, it requires hours and hours of dedicated training to reach the level of performance that we need from a dog to ensure that game is not wasted. We simply can't buy a Lab pup, raise it in our living rooms while it plays with Frisbees and tennis balls, and expect the dog to perform in the field. Since the breed has a natural affinity for retrieving, it will likely pursue downed game, but it may just as easily retrieve a decoy as the downed game we want and then may run off with the decoy and chew it to bits!

On the other hand, we could spend equal hours training our poodles and achieve some good results, but the conditions in the field wouldn't bode well for the animal. It may just look at you with eyes that say: "*I am not going in that cold water. Get your own duck!*" (Therein lies the old adage: "If you want a job done right, do it yourself!") A Lab, on the other hand, will eagerly respond, which is just what we want in our employees! Hiring and developing dedicated employees results in similar satisfaction to raising a hunting pup—spending hours training it with love and discipline and then watching it retrieve your bird on a cold fall day in the field.

3. Measuring performance against objectives

As we learned from Mr. Webster, *goals* are critical to our measuring and recruiting efforts. What's your goal? I ask that question of my employees a lot.

I often get this response, "I want to make a lot of money."

"Is that *really* your goal?" I will ask in retort.

"Well, no, I really want to travel."

"OK, then you want *financial security* and *leisure time,* and not necessarily wealth."

I then go on to show them that clarifying their goal is the first step to attainment of it.

The most frequent response I receive when I ask for a goal is this… "I don't know what my goal is."

Well, if they don't yet know where they want to be, you can help direct them, which fits nicely into creating the ***growth relationship***.

Mapping goals is made up of three distinct aspects:

M = measurable. Without a yardstick, how do we know our progress?

A = achievable. We must be able to get where we want to go.

P = profitable. Doing busywork doesn't help us to be better off. (*Profitable* also means *for the company* and not simply for the employee.)

A MAP refers to a strategic method of goal setting. Using a MAP can make a lot of difference in job satisfaction, because you and the employee can both *see* improvement. It also makes performance appraisals simple to conduct, because you both know where the employee said they'd be at the conclusion of a task or function. You must take subjectivity out of the appraisal equation or it will lead to frustration for both of you. I disliked the appraisal system until I established clearly defined objectives that each employee developed so we both knew their accomplishments and frailties. (I always retain veto power over any objective.)

An example of a well thought out objective for a flight attendant may be as follows:

Goal = Increase repeat business for the airline by two percent

M = Measure results by customer satisfaction ratings each quarter

A = Achievable through increasing the efficiency of in-flight operations

P = Improves overall revenue goals of the company

Once the outline is produced, we need to develop key aspects that will assist in its attainment. For example, outline the necessary steps to success:

1. How will the flight attendant increase repeat business?

   By improving customer satisfaction and loyalty.

2. How is that measured by management?

   Using satisfaction ratings to be tabulated quarterly.

3. Why is this profitable?

   Can improve revenue by retaining frequent travelers and filling aircraft.

The manager must be cognizant of the aspects of the flight that may impact customer satisfaction. For example, delayed flights aren't within the scope of an attendant's role unless they involve delayed departures due to a cabin being unprepared for takeoff. That *is* within the scope of an attendant's role. A step within the "acheivable" category of the goal may be to ensure that passengers have stowed their belongings and are properly seated well before the captain is prepared to takeoff. No matter the order of the steps, I hope you see the method to be used in establishing goals.

An unacceptable goal may read as follows:

Goal = Prepare meals and effectively distribute them to passengers

Why is that not an acceptable goal? Because it's a *function* of the attendant's position, not a profitable goal for the position. It's what they're *supposed* to do. If we simply add the words *within three minutes to the goal* then it becomes a performance goal that can be measured and will result in improved efficiency.

> **Distinguish *objectives* from *tasks* in order to keep your employees contributing to the company's success—and ultimately to their own.**

In general, employees need to feel useful and that their efforts contribute to the organization. That, of course, means that the company must also have clearly defined goals, a plan to improve, and ways to measure that improvement and to ensure that it can be attained and is profitable. Too many companies have blanket objectives, like "Improve sales by twenty-eight percent this fiscal year."

The first question employees ask is, "OK, how are we going to do that?"

If it's achievable, tell them how you're going to do it and that progress will be measured often to ensure the company is on-track. Perhaps a new national ad campaign is to be developed that will cost millions of dollars. Let your employees know so that their contributions matter to the goal's success. (Later on, we'll look at priorities, so keep setting goals firmly in your mind to understand their relationship to each other.)

On with the hunt...

I arrived in Fairbanks on that cold fall day, Jim's manager met me at the airport. Driving to the office, we spoke in hushed tones about the weather, the office, his new girlfriend, and just about anything other than Jim's termination. It was an uncomfortable meeting. The manager showed signs that he didn't want to confront Jim, (unfortunately, that's part of being a manager). His behavior led me to nagging doubts about the mission at hand. Perhaps Jim wasn't totally at fault, after all. Perhaps we should have been looking at the manager's results, too.

Good questions, but it wasn't to be. Jim had been hung out there for firing. He was the fall guy for negative fiscal results. The problem, of course, was that Jim wasn't directly responsible for all of the results in question. Nonetheless, Jim was getting the boot! To say that Jim was surprised by our action would be an understatement.

I quietly evaluated our position for firing him and it came down to a simple rule: He'd been an effectual manager for a smaller department, but he just didn't show the talent to manage on the larger scale. We'd made a mistake in his assignment. We had broken the **Big 1**: *Hire the right people for the job.* Unfortunately for Jim, he paid for our failure.

After Jim's termination, I spoke again to the manager in a private meeting.

"Why did Jim have so much trouble managing this operation?" I asked while sipping stale coffee from a paper cup.

The manager had no good reasons, only excuses. I looked around his office: papers and notebooks strewn about carelessly on dusty shelves, a large computer sat askew on the corner of his big black desk, and he tapped his fingers nervously to some mental music.

"How much time did you spend preparing him for this assignment?"

WHACK! Like being hit in the teeth by an errant tree branch, I was slammed by **BIG 2.**

2.
TRAINING and EDUCATION

While Jim didn't have the natural talent to handle an office roughly double the size of his previous one, he also hadn't received adequate training before assuming his duties. Whose fault was that?

> *Assuming that prior education is enough preparation for an employee.* Sometimes when we hire an employee, we base our decision on their level of education. We assume that a college graduate has more ability than a high school graduate. I'm not knocking higher education, but education alone isn't a foregone conclusion when it comes to hiring or reassigning an employee to a job.

Previous education is important, but even more important is the amount and effectiveness of corporate training. Take, for example, the employee who has a lot of reading to do as part of their job. Having an English degree indicates probable proficiency, but it doesn't indicate that they'll comprehend the material required by the job.

Conducting a pre-employment test would be helpful to determine aptitude. If you select that approach, the test should be developed on roughly an eighth-grade level. Additionally, you must assure that there are no discriminatory elements in your test. It may be best to use a professional resource to conduct such tests for your organization.

There are at least three different styles of tests out in the market today:

Knowledge based: tests the candidate's knowledge of the job task

Performance based: tests the candidate's ability to perform the task

Psychological test: test the candidate's mental conditioning to do the task

Like the poodle, it's better to test them before going hunting!

What is *training*? Well, let's see what Webster has to say about it: *"To form the habits, thoughts, or behavior of by discipline and instruction."* WOW! Right on target. *"Instruction: the knowledge imparted."* Instructing deals with telling someone how to do something, while "discipline" forms thoughts, habits, and behavior. Training is exactly what the doctor ordered for our employees. We don't just want to tell them how to do a task, do we? No, we want and NEED to form their behavior and habits to OUR satisfaction while they're performing the task. Formulating a training program, no matter how complex the job, is absolutely necessary to ensure that an employee meets our expectations. How can they possibly perform if they aren't shown how we want the job done?

Assuming that our employees know what we want and how we want it.

For example, don't say, "Prepare a report for me indicating our position in the marketplace."

Rather, say, "Using current trends indicated in industry trades, compare them to our fiscal report of last year. Prepare a detailed report outlining our position with respect to other *like* businesses in our market. I'll need the report no later than next week. Prepare an outline by tomorrow and we'll review it together to ensure that it meets the needs for upper management's evaluation. Do you understand what I want?

Do you see the difference? We set our needs, what data to use, the steps to use, our timeline, what the information is for, and we ensure that they understand by allowing them to ask questions. Additionally, it allows them to use their innovation to create the outline, thereby showing that you have confidence in them and that they contribute to the success of the project. Big difference in expectations, and the results will much better reflect our intentions.

You may wonder if you have to say all of that every time you ask for a report. The answer is no. Once you and your employee understand the parameters of the report, and AS LONG AS THEY DON'T CHANGE, requesting the report AND outlining timelines should be adequate. Different reports require different instructions. Stay flexible.

Develop a training program, which begins with a position analysis indicating the functions that are necessary for the position. Test frequently throughout the program to assure the students understanding. When you describe the job requirements to a candidate, you may hear, "Oh, I've done that sort of thing in college or at my previous job." Ignore that as a reason to hire the candidate. Just because they've done it elsewhere doesn't mean they'll do it the way YOU want it done in your organization, unless they can provide examples of their earlier work for your perusal. Asking for examples of previous work can also provide you with some ideas about how other companies or institutions address similar tasks—good method to review your own.

So, now you've laid out the position analysis to use as a guideline in developing your training. Good. Let's work with the flight attendant again.

BASIC POSITION ANALYSIS - FLIGHT ATTENDANT

Task	Duration	Skills or Knowledge required
Standing	Constant	Balance
Food service	Two hours	Food service training Health and safety training
Safety instruction	15 min.	Safety training, public speaking intercom use, demonstration
Customer service	Constant	Positive demeanor, excellent communication skills, knowledge of flight schedules, problem resolution, systems knowledge
Emergency procedures	Spontaneous	Emergency training, self-control, excellent communication skills
Bending, lifting	Occasionally	Able to lift 40 lbs overhead

Training required for this position:

Program	Duration	Resource	Topics
Food service	Eight hours	Internal	Oven use Safe food handling Cart securement
Oven use	One hour	On location	Safe use
Safe food handling	Two hours	Safety Department	Health

The training outline should be as detailed as necessary, but can be done on the back of a napkin, if that's where the ideas strike you. The development stage can be simple. Some actual hands-on training may be discounted if the employee can demonstrate proficiency during a *performance evaluation*. For example, if you observed an employee on another airline and recruited them to work for your airline, they've demonstrated their aptitude to you and you may be able to displace otherwise required training, as long as their demonstration meets the performance you expect. Let's face it, employees have a tendency to streamline the steps necessary to perform a function once they've begun to do it on a regular basis. DO NOT dismiss that tendency as *laziness*. Sometimes the simpler steps they use can lead to great new efficiencies for your company. Be careful to correctly decipher the difference.

The pit crew...

For those of you who have watched a professional car race at the track, you'll undoubtedly know where I'm going with this. Pit crews are highly trained members of a race team that each have a *specific* task to perform. While the tasks are different and unique to that crewmember, all tasks support the whole—to win the race. When a team wins a race, what do they do? CELEBRATE!

How much celebration does your organization do when you win a contract, add a new client, or exceed customer expectations? Those are all goals within your ultimate purpose—to create a thriving, profitable business with staying power.

Can you imagine being a crewmember on a winning team? The elation must be overwhelming to see it all come together for the goal. Guess what the crew does next—train! Why? *To do it faster the next time!* They don't sit on their success and say, "Hey, guys, we've achieved our goal so we can relax now!" NO, they begin evaluating what they did right and what they did wrong and how to do it better the next time.

Through the evaluation process, new tools may be designed, new techniques developed, new products enlisted, a complete reengineering of their process may also occur. They work tirelessly in their review of the task so they can shave a second off the overall process—even tenths of seconds can make a difference between first and second. By the way, practice takes place before the race. It's all about the preparation. What do you think the second place team is doing—and the third place team, and the last place team? Training, training, repetition, repetition, evaluating, and evaluating. Why? Because they WANT to win races! Each team member must complete their assigned task flawlessly and as fast as possible. There are few second chances to get it right, and the result of poor performance can be deadly.

Imagine instilling such awe-inspiring desire within your company. You'd be well on your way to developing the kind of business you want to operate. Take some lessons from the pit crew. Watch carefully the next time you see a race and identify the assigned tasks, aligned with proven talent. By the way, if they have a crewmember who can't change a tire in the allotted time, they either work with them until they can or they replace them! Terminating non-productive employees may sometimes be your only option, but only after fair opportunities have been given, with clear and concise directions on what they must do and how.

Managers should behave as *mechanics*. Automobiles are resources for our business, just as employees are. A mechanic painstakingly cares for the automobiles in a fleet. They're qualified, dedicated, and vigilant to ensure that the fleet vehicles are safe and reliable—and capable of taking the sales team to their next big sale! What may happen if the car breaks down on a trip to see the client you've all wanted to land? As mechanics care for cars, managers should care for employees. That is to say, they must be qualified, have the right tools, the dedication, and vigilance to ensure that employees perform at their top capacity. Even though we provide maintenance, like automobiles, employees occasionally malfunction—but as we do for the auto, we repair the cause and keep an eye on the problem to ensure that we've fixed it! We simply don't send it to the wrecking yard!

NOTE: Safety training can't be displaced. It's mandatory in most industries that ALL employees attend detailed training for their health and safety. There should never be shortcuts when their safety, or the safety of your customers, is involved! Safety and health training should be its own category within your training outline. In the case of our flight attendant, much of what an attendant does is for safety's sake AND required by the governing agency.

> **Asking for a portfolio that outlines a candidate's previous experience during an interview will help you evaluate their experience and knowledge level. In some cases, it may limit the amount of training you deem necessary and can provide you with some innovative ideas to try at your company.**

A *training needs assessment* should be drafted to determine the level of training necessary for a specified type of candidate. Once you've developed the pool of candidates, identify their experience level for the tasks at hand. Some candidates will have the talents, training, and experience, while others may only have raw talent. A simplified assessment grid will resemble this example:

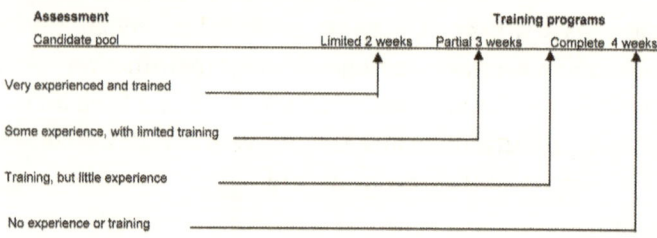

Using this grid, you can determine the level of training needed for specific employees, based on your impressions from testing or interviewing. If you need employees in a hurry, hire those who can get to work fastest. If you have the luxury of time, hire those candidates who may take more training.

A sound policy is to hire employees for your *training program* with recruitment into full employment based on their successful completion of the training objectives. This approach reduces a lot of the hassles you'll face terminating new employees who don't meet the basic training requirements. You have NOT hired these applicants as employees, but as *trainees*, with a specific objective to meet in order to be considered for full employment. This allows time to assess their capabilities.

Now may a good time for me to discuss what I consider to be the great plague of American industry—*apathy*. Apathetic employees will do more harm to your organization than good if you're simply plugging a vacancy by keeping a *body*. Apathy leads to failure. There's nothing good that ever comes from it.

Mr. Webster defines **apathy** as *"A lack of concern or interest."* Do your employees appear to have a lack of concern or interest? How do you deal with it? First try to identify the source; poor job performance can be caused by a lack of training or ability. It can also be caused by rebellion. What if they are simply lazy? *Lazy* employees are one thing, but *apathetic* employees can do much more harm! Apathy can also come from under-utilizing a person's talents, resulting in an employee feeling *pigeonholed* without the possibility of advancement. We see this a lot in senior personnel when they finally realize that they've reached the top rung for their position. Remember Jim's manager? He had become complacent in his job. It was evident by the condition of his office, the dust on the equipment, and the work strewn about. He simply didn't care about the organization any longer, much less his employees. Unfortunately one of the only methods to deal with apathy is to get personal! Find out what the problem is! (As far as I'm concerned, the law has rung all of the emotion out of the workplace, like we would ring water from wet socks. Like it or not, there *is* an emotional balance that can be achieved in the workplace and has real value for improving job performance.) Apathy generally leads to poor behavior. We recognize apathy by <u>observing behavior</u>.

> Training is necessary for performance, but to energize employee *purpose*, it's how we *treat* them, not how we *train* them!

"But I don't have enough time to watch all of them," you may counter. "I pay them don't I? Why isn't *that* enough to ensure that they perform?"

Water seeks its own level. Employees place a value on their contribution to the company, but management may place a different value on the employee's contribution. An employee will contribute a proportionate level of labor to the task compared to how they feel they're being rewarded. As we all know, *rewards* are not always financial—they can come in as many different forms as you have different personalities working for you. Explore ideas and through observation you may find the rewards that make your employees tick. PRESTO! We have **BIG 3**.

BIG 3

3.
SUPERVISION

Before we get into supervision, let's quickly review what we have discovered along the trail: we've identified the tasks to be performed, recruited employees with the talent to do the job, and we've trained them. All well and good, right? Wrong! All of that will be of little use unless we observe our employees' performance and provide feedback.

Observation and feedback go hand in hand. Observation alone is like having one bookend. It requires a follow-up mechanism for it to be effectual. Therein lies one of the *great* rules of management: *Employees do what we inspect, not what we expect.* Take a moment to let that sink in.

Although Watson shadowed Sherlock Holmes religiously, he did not have the same detective skills and here is what Sherlock told him: "Watson, you do not *see* because you do not **look**, and when you do *look*, you do not **reason** from what you see."

As Holmes teaches us, we must reason from the clues we detect when watching employee performance!

The smelly dog theory...

OK, let's discuss what I mean by that *great* rule. Management must have a mechanism whereby it reviews job performance—often. Imagine a student without a test or quiz. How would their performance and knowledge be properly evaluated? You know those little scraps of paper that read "Inspected by #10" that fall out of your newly purchased shoes? That's what this section is all about— observing and providing feedback to keep employees doing the job as we expect. Employees won't perform their duties correctly by osmosis. It takes meaningful supervision to keep them on track. In some organizations, a third party department, such as a safety department or quality control department, performs inspection and evaluation. While effectual and meaningful in production or service type companies, that type of evaluation may not be applicable in your company.

That brings up another topic of inspecting performance. I call it "the smelly dog theory." The theory is built upon the premise that a third party inspector brings *fresh eyes* to the function. In other words, we often don't know our dog smells until we go away for a while and then return home to find that our dog, otherwise smelling fresh as a daisy, now smells, well, like a dog. For the sake of clarity, we'll use the term *desensitized*. You may have experienced a loss of sensitivity when eating garlic or onions. After a while, we lose our ability to distinguish the pungent odor that emanates from those foods. To demonstrate the phenomenon, try eating a garlic sauté while your partner eats something without garlic. Your love life may suffer a bit, but you'll clearly understand my point. The smelly dog theory applies in almost all types of tasks or functions. That theory isn't what this section is about, but it may provide you with some insights about seeking outside assistance for your organization.

The obvious question you may ask is, "Don't my employees know when they're performing inadequately?"

Maybe, but maybe not. The point is that YOU know they're performing incorrectly, and if *you* know, then you have an obligation to tell *them* so. (Think back to the first failure that I noted: *our employees not knowing how we think they're performing*. Rigorous supervision  eliminates that failure.) Sometimes our employees may not want us supervising them so closely, especially when it turns into *micro-management*. We must be careful to separate those two types of performance inspection. Micro-management is the infinitesimal inspection of tiny bits and pieces. Sometimes micro-management misses the big picture, because we're too enthralled with the itsy-bitsy aspects of performance to see the progress our employees are making. That type of evaluation often leads more to mistrust and animosity than to performance improvement, which is what this book is all about. There are different objectives for the two, so be careful not to fall into the trap of micro-management, unless it's absolutely necessary for the success of the organization.

Supervise employees by providing feedback, direction and encouragement.

I speak to employees from all different types of companies, and I often hear something like this: "My boss must think I'm doing a good job because I never see her!

I also hear, "My boss is always on my back to produce, but really doesn't understand what I do."

The most common remark is, "My boss is too busy or seldom available."

Do any of those declarations sound familiar? Do any of those comments depict what supervision is all about?

Very rarely do I hear, "My boss monitors and provides useful feedback on a timely basis."

 I learned long ago, when I used to train horses, that a trainer must discipline immediately when misbehavior is detected. Otherwise, the animal forgets why it's being disciplined. When that happens, rebellion rears its ugly head and a swift kick by a steel-shod horse quickly refines your training technique.

If you caught it earlier, you'll note that I also introduced the word *discipline* into the supervision template. That word was introduced when we were deciding on the differences between *training* and *instructing*. Do you recall the definition of *training* I referenced earlier? If not, here it is again: *"To form the habits, thoughts, or behavior of by discipline and instruction."* Do you see the word discipline in there? There's a definite place in all organizations for discipline. It's a vital part of your continuous training of employees. Isn't that what **supervision** is really all about? Well, let's see: *Supervise: "To watch over and direct (work or workers), to oversee." Oversee: "To supervise or manage."* Now let's follow this through to the conclusion. *Manage*: *"To take or be in charge or control of. To dominate or influence, especially by tact."* Well, how else will you influence your employees than to supervise their activity and provide them with feedback, both positive and negative? Remember, a pat on the back is only eighteen inches higher than a kick in the pants!

Employees learn bad habits and behavior from other employees, not from the company! *Unacceptable behavior* that goes uncorrected becomes *acceptable behavior.* If a manager allows poor behavior by one employee, then all other employees will assume the poor performance or behavior is acceptable. If your *policy* states that employees MUST be on time for work, but your *practice* is to allow some flexibility, then the practice becomes the policy. Attempting to enforce the policy with one—if your practice is different for others—can lead to trouble, including discrimination claims.

No matter what type of disciplinary program you elect for your employees, it must be applied fairly and consistently, with the intent to improve behavior or performance. The only way we truly know what type of discipline to enact is to inspect what our employees are doing, and that means to *supervise* them. Tell them when they're bad and tell them when they're good. Employees want to know where they stand with you, good and bad.

Farmer Jones...

At one time in my career, I lived in Ohio and I learned a valuable lesson, taught to me by an old farmer. He was sunburned brown and tough as a steel cable. He was planning to hire some help for chores about his large farm. I suggested that he put a notice up in the local drugstore, since I'd seen several adolescents hanging out there with nothing better to do than to make a racket with their skateboards.

In a steely voice, chiseled by experience, he said, "<u>Hire a boy, you have a boy; hire two boys and you have half a boy; hire three boys and you have no boy at all.</u>" Then he turned and limped away.

On that humid summer day, I learned a real lesson from someone who'd obviously lived it. One employee, closely supervised, can provide more work than multiple employees who, left unsupervised, may end up playing around all day, producing little effort and less effect on objectives. The key, of course, isn't how many employees one has, but how well they're monitored and influenced to perform their intended functions.

By way of example, in Jim's case he didn't get the benefit of learning our evaluation of his work. He got the hammer, the big stick, the final curtain, the door out. Too bad for him, and for all of the other employees he worked with. There's no better way to stop apathy than to observe and correct misbehavior. I've seen employees spend most of their working day trying to bring attention to a worker who they felt wasn't performing their job. Remember, water seeks its own level. Our employees want to know that we're treating them all fairly and disciplining the weak links within the company. Never side with an employee against another! It's a management no-no and will get you into trouble. You must keep all correction confidential and professional. When you make notes in the employee file, avoid references to personal issues, such as "Y doesn't meet our standards because she dresses like a slob." Rather, say, "Y isn't meeting our grooming standards" or "I've observed Y on several occasions out of uniform or dress code." Never put a warning or disciplinary note into an employee file until you've spent the time to speak to them and to attempt to influence proper behavior.

Improving employee performance, and ultimately corporate margins, depends largely on supervision. Let's face it. The company pays you to manage your employees and they have the right to expect that you're fulfilling that critical role in a professional manner. I propose that many companies could meet objectives with fewer employees if the supervisors of that organization adopted **BIG 3**.

> Employees only learn how they're doing during their annual performance appraisal. By then, it's already too late to make a positive difference in their work product. Consider waiting a whole year to tell your partner, spouse or children how you feel they are doing!

Supervision of employees is easy when you're there with them every day, but what do we do about those outside of the normal business environment? Outside sales representatives immediately come to mind. How do you know they're representing your organization to clients the way you want them to? A simple little trick is to have the outside salesperson sell *you*! In other words, ask them to come in and conduct a mock sales meeting, with you as the client. You'll quickly learn how they represent your business and it will also allow you to provide coaching and counselling as you participate in the effort. It will benefit them as you work with them and will also provide you with the peace of mind you need. Customer surveys and "secret shoppers" are also methods you can use to measure employee performance when you're not there to view it firsthand. EVERY group of employees should have some form of service rating by an independent or unassociated third party so you can objectively measure performance. Remember though that this measures product not behaviour.

The name game...

The following are some monikers that describe various manager types:

✓ **Dragon Lady** = tyrannical. Uses pain and belittling remarks. Assumes total authorship of all departmental production. Stifles ownership and innovation.

✓ **Void Lloyd** = too busy to deal with supervision. Employees often left to their own devices. Production suffers.

✓ **Friendly Fred** = too concerned with how they're viewed by employees to act as a boss. Easily coerced by employees. Production often off-target.

✓ **Crisis Chris** = literally everything is a crisis. Pushes employees hard to perform in stressful environment. High turnover. Projects often incomplete.

✓ **The General** = commands employees to charge forward, even with inadequate resources to achieve the task at hand. Will sacrifice employees to meet objectives—and they know it. Disregards caution and moves ahead against the odds. Experiences turnover and worker compensation claims.

✓ **Mom (or Dad, Uncle, Aunt, Granny, etc.)** = parental influence. Feels obligated to correct ideals. Overprotective. Has a tendency toward favoritism. Baby-sits and rarely considers employee suggestions. May promote in fighting. Feels that they alone have more rights than less tenured employees.

✓ **Pompous Pat** = too good for everything and everyone. Brownnoser to senior management. Sacrifices employees at will to gain personal ground with seniors. Mistrusted by employees. Selects only high profile work and claims credit.

✓ **Slimy Sam** = too personal. Enough said.

No matter how fair you think you are with employees, you may have a nickname that bespeaks their feelings about you. You just have to find out what it is and WHY it is. What perception do your employees have of you? A moniker is usually an indicator of how our employees think we manage. Though often humorous, nicknames may accurately depict how our employees rate us, with specific and painful detail.

It's time to look at practical supervision of employees. We'll take the flight attendant again as an example. Having determined that she was performing her job to our expectation and that our customers were pleased with her methods, what should we say?

"Good work, Z, the customers are pleased with your efforts and so is the company. You're a great example to your fellow employees."

If you thought Z was happy about her job before, she'll really be flying high now! She knows she's doing the job correctly and she's happy doing it, but she wants and NEEDS to know that you agree she's an exceptional employee. Such feedback validates her own belief that she's performing the tasks, *as you want them done.* But doesn't such a honey-dripping pat on the back seem over the top? Not to Z, it doesn't, and she *wants* that sort of feedback from her employer.

Thinking of the flight attendant, I must tell you about another list of ideas I formed on that long flight. As I watched her perform her duties, I was impressed with her apparent delight with the company. Adjusting my air valve to cool down my writing hand, I asked if she liked working for the company. With a nod of her gray curls and a smile, she replied in the affirmative.

"Have you worked here a long time?" I inquired further.

"Nineteen years," was her *isn't that impressive* answer.

Yes, it was impressive. I thought to myself that it seems harder and harder to find employees who'll make a career out of a job. It seems that we've become a society of vagabonds, traversing the industrial landscape in search of greener pastures. I often find that money doesn't dictate a greener pasture for the employee. It's more frequently a negative work environment that prompts them to look elsewhere. A positive atmosphere, with honest feedback and supervisors who are genuinely interested in their employees' success make up a positive work environment. Donuts and soda can only do so much to entice an employee's loyalty.

> **Thrill in your employees' successes, not in their failures.**

The bill of rights...

So, there I was, chatting with the flight attendant and the reasons she liked the company. I sipped more coffee and began two new lists titled: *"What does the company have the right to expect from its employees?"* and *"What does the employee have the right to expect from their employer?"* (I'm sure you think those are basic questions that have been asked and answered a million times before, starting with the very first employee, but do you really think managing people was any different then? HOW we managed them was different, but I'm sure they had the same basic needs that employees have today: shelter, food, security, and a nurturing environment.)

Did you notice that I used the words *right to expect*? Here are some synonyms of what I mean:

> ➢ **Just   Deserved   Proper   Ethical   Good   Fair   Merited**

I know those words may sound old-fashioned, but they're words that a company AND its employees can rightfully use. In today's *give-me-all-you-got-and-as-fast-as-possible-or-I-will-leave* world, *right* doesn't seem to have much value. Remember, the reason many employees feel the need to stray is largely a work environment issue, not a monetary issue. Be careful, and woe to those of you who misinterpret my meaning. *Monetary fairness* is a major issue in turnover, but if like-jobs are paid roughly the same, that shouldn't produce unhappy employees unless they're paid substantially below the competitive wage for the industry or the employee's responsibilities.

Here's my list on **rights**:

EMPLOYEE RIGHT	EMPLOYER RIGHT
Competitive wages and benefits	Consistent performance
Safe and healthy environment	Honesty
Fair labor practices	Loyalty
Job security	Support of objectives
Loyalty	Efficiency
	Ethical

The list went on, but what do you see on both of them? LOYALTY. *Loyalty* floated to the top, like cream rises from milk. Your *best* employees may rise from the body, not from without. It seems we feel compelled to search for talent outside, when it may be right in front of us every day. As managers, we've heard time and time again that the *new* employees of today have little to no loyalty. I'm certain you're familiar with the term *Generation X*. Some management gurus (I'm not arguing their right to call themselves that) claim that the kids of today have no loyalty to a company.

"Why, we just can't find loyal employees."

WOW! That opinion has been as overcooked as the first Thanksgiving turkey I roasted. There are numerous books out on that subject, so I won't delve into the fray, but I would offer this: Loyalty is *earned*, just like *respect* is earned. (Don't forget, the **BIG 1** implies that it's our responsibility to hire the *right* people for the job.) Loyalty begets loyalty. The problem with new workers today is NOT with their loyalty. It's that *we* don't understand *their* cause. Once you can pinpoint their cause, building loyalty isn't any different for them than anyone else. What are some causes to consider? A healthy environment is important, as are flexible work hours, continuing education, innovation, leadership and many other factors. There aren't necessarily more issues today, just different issues. The last thing I'll say on the subject (because I promised I wouldn't belabor the issue) is this: *Get over it!* Generation X isn't the future—it's NOW. They're already in our workplaces and NOW is the time to establish a mutual loyalty! It may require a different way of thinking, but you can do it if you're committed to making it happen.

I must address something that's hot off the griddle today. There are camps that suggest that corporate America doesn't want or need loyal employees—it wants and needs *elastic* employees. As a manager in a major corporation, I DO want loyal employees. I won't have to continue recruiting new people if the employees I have are performing their functions the way *I want them* performed. (The first question you have to address is whether your way to do the task is the best way to do the task.) Perhaps that requires some flexibility in employees, but it also requires commitment, dedication, training, talent, supervision, innovation, and integrity. There isn't a *single* adjective that fully describes all of the attributes of the *right* employee, whether it's "loyal" or "flexible," because the *rooms* in this house have different purposes. Unless I want all of my employees to do everything (the buzzword now is *multi-task*), then I will discriminately select them for their natural talents and model them into an employee who meets my expectations. That's the challenge of management.

Creating ownership among your employees is also a great way to establish loyalty. There's no easier way to create ownership than to simply give your employees the credit for the product they generate. Why do so many managers feel compelled to take credit for their employees' work product? Insecurity? Perhaps, but that may tell us that the manager doesn't feel recognized by the company. **They** may be having a problem with loyalty. Allegiance goes all the way up and down in a progressive work environment.

I speak to many companies about employees and it often seems that the company *rights* usually outweighs what they're willing to give in return. Employment is a balance, just like any successful relationship.

I'd be remiss if I failed to address the potential side effects of too much supervision. I'm not referring to micro-management. Supervising too much may include some of the following examples:

> ➢ Multiple reviews of the same project (this may also indicate a change in the project from its inception,

OR that your employees aren't producing first time finals, OR that you're confused about what you want).

➢ Directing every aspect of a project from the most simple to the most complicated.

➢ Overemphasizing your authority by belaboring simple day-to-day work rules, etc.

The dangers associated with over-supervising may fall into one of these categories:

➢ The manager takes on more of the employee's duties.

➢ The manager becomes responsible for EVERY decision, no matter how notable.

➢ Employees don't feel trusted.

➢ Innovation may be stifled.

➢ Employees will only do what they are asked (little to no ownership in the organization or function).

As we close out the discussion regarding the first **BIG THREE**, it may be obvious to you that if we had only these three principles to work with, we could make vast and positive improvements for our organizations, but there's still more to discover. All of the hiring, training, and supervising we do will never be enough if we don't provide our employees with adequate resources to perform their tasks. Ahoy, **Big 4.**

BIG 4

4.

Adequate Resources

This problem seems to be a catchall in many corporations today. Do we ever hear the end of "I need more staff, I need more time, I need more money, I need a faster computer?" The problems associated with resources are hard to nail down. In many cases, the employees are correct—they DO need more—but having more doesn't necessarily improve performance. It only means that they have more—not that they have as much as they require to meet your expectations. On the other hand, employees can't meet their job requirements without adequate resources. The problem then becomes what is *adequate* and what is *excessive*? It's a question that only you can answer, and it depends largely upon your company's anticipated growth and current demands.

While there never seems to be an end to the "I need" syndrome, there are tools that you can use to determine factually whether or not the demands are legitimate. The process begins at the position analysis stage and carries though supervision. For example, do you recall the report we asked our employee to compile earlier? Let's review the possible resource issues by asking some questions about our expectations for the product:

"Using current trends indicated in industry trades, compare them to our fiscal report of last year. Prepare a detailed report outlining our position with respect to other *like* businesses in our market. I'll need the report no later than next week. Prepare an outline by tomorrow and we'll review it together to ensure that it meets my needs for upper management's evaluation. Do you understand what I want?"

OK, you know what you want from the employee, but what will they need to complete it to your satisfaction? Ask yourself:

1. Will I accept the report drafted in pencil on a legal pad?
2. Will I accept the report in typed fashion?
3. Should it include a spreadsheet comparison to *like* businesses in our industry?
4. Am I going to want multiple copies?
5. Will this necessitate a computer or word processor?
6. Do they need access to industry trade publications and if so, will they have to purchase them or are they readily available?
7. Can the employee handle the report alone, or will they need the assistance of others?
8. Does the employee have the TIME to complete the report, forsaking all other duties?

9. How much of my time will it require to review the outline and do I have the time to give? (Your time is a principal resource necessary for employee growth.)

Let's assume that the employee has access to a computer/word processor, they have the time and trade publications—all of the tools necessary to prepare a report. TIME and TALENT become the ultimate tests of task performance. TALENT isn't a resource problem (unless they need the input of other staff personnel), so TIME becomes our biggest concern. If you think about it, we're ALL faced with the dilemma of inadequate time. Time *management* requires accurately prioritizing the demands of the job. How does one prioritize the demands they're faced with—and leave adequate time to handle other projects outside of their normal duties?

As an example, I have learned to outline all of the common duties that my employees deal with on a daily basis. I then prioritize those duties for them and that helps them deal with the issues they face, because they don't have to ask what they should do first. Let's look at the flight attendant for an example of that:

List the duties:	Priority:
Safety of passengers and crew	1
Assisting passengers with seating and carry-on stowage	1
Prepare and serve meals	2
Prepare and serve beverages	2

Make safety announcements	1
Assist passengers with scheduling questions	3
Pass out reading materials	4
Chitchat with guests	4
Serve meals and beverages to pilots	3

Priority matrix:

1. Absolute
2. Must do, but not at the risk of #1
3. Should do, but not at the risk of #1 or #2
4. Only as time allows

Concerning my target Jim, inadequate resources were part of his dilemma. He didn't have the support staff or time to do all that was required of him. Whose fault was that? His manager's, of course. Jim wasn't in a position to acquire the necessary resources, BUT he was responsible to bring those needs to his manager's attention.

Often, my employees tell me that they have too much work to do, based on my priority system. I handle that complaint by reducing the projects that are assigned to the employee. This has a threefold effect:

✓ It sends the message that I'm willing to reduce the requirements to meet the employee's talent.

✓ It heads off the next logical complaint that the employee feels underpaid.

✓ I reassign more duties to a more capable employee, thereby creating an aura of competition, encouraging the complainer to work smarter.

In the unlikely event that I have an employee who just can't cut it, it also provides documentation in my file that I've limited the workload at the request of the employee. They have a hard time arguing that I've simply pulled work away from them due to some personality conflict. (A side benefit is that often the employee who picks up additional duties, feels *recognized* for their ability. I kill two birds with one stone.) I'm very careful how I handle it. Otherwise, I might end up with two complainers, *both* suggesting that they have too much work.

We'll now review a resource template to illustrate *resources* vs. *performance* objectives. We'll use the hapless flight attendant again for this purpose.

Formula = PC*AS/TA = Resources required

Meal Service Resource Template				
Passenger Count (PC)	Time Allowed (TA)	Service to Passenger Allowance (One pax per minute of allowed time)	Average Service Time per Passenger (AS)	Resources Required
120	120 min.	1 to 1	1 pax in 5 min.	5
100	120 min.	1 to .8	1 pax in 5 min.	4
75	120 min.	1 to .6	1 pax in 5 min.	3

For example – 120 passengers served at five minutes per passenger would take 600 minutes to serve. With only 120 minutes available for service, we would need five crewmembers to serve in the allotted time or we can reduce the amount of time per passenger service or increase allowable time. By reducing the pax count, we serve in less time using fewer resources.

Discussing resources, we should consider common everyday issues to better understand this principal. Do you have a favorite sports team? For the sake of argument, let's choose basketball. When our team doesn't win the finals, we blame the players, the coach, and the team's administration.

We may say to ourselves, "If only we'd only acquired so-and-so, our team would be much better."

We tend to look at it as being the team's administrative failure for not securing adequate players to ensure victory. Sometimes we blame the players themselves for not playing better. How does a player play better than their natural ability? Training and practice. Furthermore, one strong player can offset the weakness of another player. Look at Michael Jordon, an obvious choice for discussion. Many people believe that HE alone carried the Bulls to their many championships. Who is to argue when looking at the Bulls' record, post-Jordon? What are the problems here? Talent, training, supervising, and resource acquisition. What about individual effort? Doesn't that count, too? Of course, and that ball bounces right into the **BIG 5**.

5.
MOTIVATION

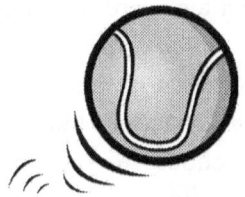

That's the way the ball bounces...

HOLY COW! *Motivations in the workplace are* words that are as difficult to explain, as they are to understand. There are all types of motivating factors to consider and that problem is likely the least quantifying of the **BIG SIX**. Trying to put a finger on motivating employees is like wrestling with the wet soap bar in the shower. Just when you think you have it, it squirts out and leaves an indent in your big toe. That's a definitive response to our efforts in motivation: sometimes our best endeavors turn around and hurt us in the end. That's why we must recruit people with the *will* to work, too.

For consistency sake, let's look at what Webster says about motivation. *Motive: "Something, as a reason or desire, acting as a spur to action."* Well, when I trained horses, I understood what a *spur* was—typically a prod to get the animal to do something it didn't want to do. That, of course, isn't how we should be motivating our employees, but we must accept the notion that sometimes pain can be a very productive method of promoting action. The problem is that the more we use pain, the more we HAVE to use pain. That alone becomes the motivating factor for the object of our attention.

If we look at the first few words of the definition provided by Webster, we see *reason* or *desire*. Those are the keys to this whole topic. Surely, a *spur* is a method we can use to promote the *reason* for action, but if we want *long-term* results, we should choose to promote *desire* to inspire action from our employees. I'd much rather the horse *want* to take me for a ride than to have to fight with the beast every tooth-chattering mile, but alas, horses are different than people. However, that doesn't mean we can learn nothing from animals when it comes to motivating methods. On the contrary, we can learn a great deal as we explore techniques to spark desire. I'm using the word *desire* to indicate that the employee *wants* to do the job well and *reasons* to mean that the employee will be compelled, by management action, to perform the job. The obvious distinction is the difference between doing the job and doing the job well. Doing the job well means that they meet or exceed our expectations and performance objectives.

In our gentler, kinder animal training world, we learn that food is a genuine method to encourage behavior. Food is a necessity of life and an excellent short-term behavior modifier. However, are we trying to modify behavior here or to develop a means to influence employee desire? Clearly, short-term modifiers have application in the work place. Bonuses, extra time off, advancement, and recognition awards can influence specific actions. Safety incentive programs are a good example of such systems.

In many companies, rewards are given for *loss-time record* improvement. That is to say that, as losses decline, rewards are received. In a nutshell, it means *give to get*. While those techniques do achieve results, they're aimed at specific, clearly defined objectives. What are some of the methods available to us in the workplace to promote *desire*?

1. Positive and enjoyable work environment
2. Employee growth and advancement opportunities
3. Loyal organization
4. Shared burden of effort by all employees, up and down
5. Salary and benefit increases/improvements
6. Security
7. Recognition for the organization (number one in their industry)
8. Sphere of influence
9. Ownership of the organizational mission

Many of those same techniques are used to provide *reasons* for performance. The difference lies in the duration of the effort and, in many cases, the quality of the product. An employee's desire to perform the job well also promotes innovation and efficiency that can improve operating profits and solidify our company's position in the marketplace. Wouldn't it be nice to find employees who performed to our expectation out of *sheer personal gratification* (SPG)? Was corporate America ever like that?

What other cultures could we use as an example of SPG? About the only group of workers who pop into my mind are the Seven Dwarfs, who whistled while they worked. In that single depiction, Walt Disney gave us a plethora of employee distinctions. Sneezy, Grumpy, Sleepy—do those characters bring to mind some of your own employees or co-workers? Why were they so happy to swing those heavy picks all day? Because it was a cartoon! (I can hear you thinking that right now.) Of course, it was a cartoon, but what could we learn from it? I learned that building a TEAM approach could be a huge motivating factor for workers.

Teams naturally indicate some form of competition— good method of influencing desire. Depending on a team's performance objectives, competition can be either a positive influence or a negative influence. We'll explore both as we review that viable technique.

As we look at developing teams, we need to recognize that it isn't for everyone or every company. TEAMS have a common goal, made up of different members contributing their unique efforts to the objective. Sometimes teams produce a bitter taste because one member is considered more valuable than another. That's a natural bi-product of a team.

When I was a child, I vividly recall the apprehension I felt as teams were selected to play ball in the recess yard at school. (I'm certain some of you have similar memories.) When I was lucky enough to have a friend picked to be a captain, I usually was selected early in the process. But when there was a captain who didn't know my abilities, I often went last in the selection process. (That was an early experience in selecting members with natural talent.) As a kid, I was tall, but skinny (oh, what happened to my waist line over the years?), so captains who weren't familiar with my ability looked at my exterior.

When developing teams in your organization and assessing the value of individual members, be certain to use previous employee evaluations as a determining factor. Although, just because an employee can display individual effort, doesn't mean they can perform as well in a team environment. Teams take a lot of effort to succeed.

Elements of a team approach (these can be good or bad):
- Common goal
- Competition
- Shared expertise
- Communication
- Peer pressure
- Efficiency
- Resource effectiveness
- Cross training
- Product quality
- Camaraderie

Some negative elements may include:

- Feelings of inadequacy
- Suppresses individual effort
- Misunderstanding of performance objectives
- Difficult to manage
- In-fighting
- Splinter groups
- "Meeting rich" and "product poor"

There are many complexities to team-building and there are many books and other resources available, should you be interested. The point I want to make is that team-building can have a positive influence on promoting an employee's *desire* to perform at their peak capacity. Like a murky swamp, however, there are dangers hidden beneath the surface that can have a negative influence, too.

Run, Bill, run!

In our efforts to develop yearning in our employees to perform their tasks to our expectations, we must carefully determine what those expectations are. When I was growing up north of Seattle, there was a boy my age that was an only child. We had lots of fun with him, calling him names, making up stories about him that were baseless—you know, typical young boy stuff. Bill was also our fall guy. He was blamed for so many things, so often, that there would have to have been six of him just to go around the neighborhood. The harder Bill tried to belong, the more we took advantage of him. Soon, the entire school thought of him as an imbecile. One particular night, my friends and I were exploring a new shopping mall that was under construction. The police showed up and spotlighted the area where we were hiding.

In an effort to throw them off our whereabouts, I whispered, "Run, Bill, Run!"

Well, you guessed it, he did run and he was caught and received a lashing when he was dropped off by a police car at home later that evening. It was undeserved, just as everything else we'd done to him over the years. Bill was simply a *nobody* in our community and could do little himself to change his potential, since it was based on how others saw him.

I went off to begin my career in Ohio and during a trip home several years later, I ran into Bill again. He'd joined the Air Force and didn't even look like the same person. Of course, he'd filled out physically, but his confidence and maturity shined. It was a true metamorphosis. I sat and talked to Bill for a while, but frankly, I was so ashamed of my behavior years earlier that I just couldn't get past the guilt that I felt. I learned some time later that Bill had died in an accident and I felt badly that I hadn't ever given him a chance to show me who he really was.

I thought about that for a long time, and I still find myself thinking of it often. The lesson I learned is this: *people seldom go beyond what other people believe about them.* That principle slashed at me like a lightning bolt when I first put it together.

You see, as long as Bill stayed around our neighborhood he couldn't disprove what we believed about him. Why? Simply because we wouldn't give him the chance—much less the time of day. When Bill joined the Air Force and moved away, he was on equal ground with all the other recruits. There were no preconceived ideas about his limitations or about who he was as a person. That new environment created an opportunity for him to reshape his life and to create a new vision of who he was to those around him. To us, he was simply Bill, the lonely kid down the street, but to his fellow military personnel, he was a strapping, knowledgeable, kind-hearted, talented, and confident man whom they thought of highly. What a difference the new environment made in his life.

As I apply that lesson to management, I always consider what my expectations are for my employees. If I expect a great deal, they'll respond accordingly, but if I expect little, I get little in return. Can we sometimes expect too much? Perhaps. If you recall, that was the question that encouraged my development of the **BIG FIVE**. Why hadn't Jim performed the way we expected? Our expectations weren't too high. It was simply that we failed to provide him with the support he needed to meet those expectations. We MUST remember to balance our expectations with talent, training, supervision, resources, and incentives.

You'll note that all five points are NOT issues for the employee to resolve—they're issues that *managers* must resolve. There isn't one point that's the responsibility of the employee. I know that many managers who read this book will disagree with that premise. Some will believe that I'm letting the employee off scot-free with no responsibility for their actions or performance. That's not what I've been attempting to imply. In the case of employee progress—meeting OUR expectations—the burden is squarely on *our* shoulders.

In this fast-paced, everything-is-a-priority corporate world, **BIG 6** plays an important role. **BIG 6** is there for you, the manager, and it helps to define the limitations of your position.

BIG 6

6.
Confused Priorities

Have you heard the phrase "good work brings more work?" Some say it differently, but you get the idea. Doing a job well sometimes results in more work. The more tasks your company assigns to you, the less time you can afford to spend on any single one. For example, do your mechanics spend as much time doing paperwork as they do servicing the company's fleet? As a manager, are you glued to your computer reading countless emails? The more spread out we become, the more difficult it is to address issues facing our employees. We become the absent manager—the one so busy with *things* that we can't take time for *people*. I trust you'll agree that working with people is more challenging—and rewarding—than working with *things*, unless your personal *natural talent* is best utilized with things.

Priorities! What a word. It signifies an order of importance. The assorted priorities addressed in **BIG 6** also suggest that we have order for each order of importance. Handling different and sometimes diverse responsibilities inevitably results in clashes between orders of importance. That means we must develop a sub-order so we can handle all of the issues relevant to the grand scheme. If that seems confusing so far, I agree. Uncertainty is a common by-product of the priority assortment model. Remember, we're talking about why employees fail to perform to our expectation—and that includes *you*.

By the time I'd arrived in Fairbanks, the outline for the **BIG FIVE** was already taking shape. I began to scrutinize the issues surrounding Jim's termination and watched for clues to my theories as the situation unfolded. As I became more enlightened, I realized that Jim was in just the predicament I had formulated.

After his termination had been hammered out, Jim wanted to see me alone. As I swung the hollow-core door shut, I directed Jim to a seat in the corner of the tiny office. The remnants of autumn sun were streaking through the shoebox-size window stuck in the corner with Picasso-like style. The room was quiet, befitting the serious nature of the situation, and the air hung in the office so thick I thought I could scrawl my name in it.

Conducting private meetings with employees was commonplace for me, and I had a pretty good idea what

I was going to hear. Rather than discarding the upcoming speech as just another *terminated employee with a bad taste in his mouth,* I decided to listen closely for signs that I was on the right track with my ideas. It isn't uncommon for an *exit conference* to produce a myriad of complaints about the company, the manager, and even personal complaints about co-workers and policies. Exit interviews can produce tremendous fact-based insights into problems at the workplace. You may also discover that the employee is absolutely right in their dissatisfaction—and you may even decide to give them another chance and assign them to a task force to address some of those issues. The key is to be inquisitive not defensive. What ownership you could create, given such an opportunity. Remember, this is about looking IN, not out.

"What happened?" Jim whispered, his head hung low between his shoulders.

I struggled for the right words to ease his obvious embarrassment, asking, "What do *you* think happened?"

I must admit that I felt guilty for Jim's demise. Perhaps I wouldn't have felt so bad, had my boss not asked me for a reason for Jim's performance, or more accurately, if I hadn't tried to answer that complex question. The meeting progressed a bit differently from that point than I'd expected, but Jim's anger was typical. He'd felt that his performance was right on track because he had *never heard otherwise from his superior.* The revenue numbers seemed solid, his subordinates appeared to perform adequately— what had been the single event that had caused his performance to be questioned? I finally recognized the probable cause. His own boss was feeding him to the lions to save his own neck.

There is an old Alaskan saying that suggests that if you intend to hike into grizzly bear country, *always hike with someone you can outrun.* By suggesting to senior management that Jim's performance was the cause of departmental problems, the manager had sidestepped his own demise and had given the company a target to aim at. Unfortunately, there are sacrifices in the corporate war.

Our meeting went on for nearly two hours. I offered responses when I felt them appropriate. Otherwise, I listened and became enlightened. I learned a great deal about the difficulties Jim had experienced in his daily tasks and had stumbled upon the **BIG SIX** as a result. Jim had been having difficulty arranging the *order of his order of importance*—his priority assortment model. His pattern would look something like this:

Training employees	Supervise two departments	Maintenance schedules	Regulatory compliance	Fleet utilization
Produce revenue	Control expenses	Prepare reports	Customer service	Vendor relationships
Human resources	Payroll	Capital issues	Sales	Policy enforcement
Hiring	Safety	Conferences	Communications	Labor disputes

Under each of those categories lay numerous priorities that had to be defined and accomplished. Some were daily, and others monthly or quarterly, with annual objectives evaluated to cover all of them. Where was Jim supposed to begin establishing the order of the order of importance?

Why hadn't his manager assisted him with that order? Which priorities were crucial? (Earlier, I showed you how I establish priorities for my staff. Left unattended, Jim had made up his own list, which, in the final analysis, had been incorrect.) I'm certain as you review Jim's model, you'll relate to many of the same issues. That's why it's important for the manager to establish the priority assortment model and the relationship of uncommon tasks or functions. It's no wonder that any employee would/could fail when faced with such a daunting task. Following are questions I asked myself: Jim likely had problems making the correct selections because of which aspects of the **BIG FIVE**?

✓ His natural talent?

Do you think that Jim had a deficiency in dealing with the issues as I've described them to you? Did he have the natural talent to manage all of the objectives required by his job?

✓ His education or training?

Did Jim bring adequate education or experience to his position? Had he been promoted too quickly within our organization? Had his manager provided hands-on training on how to deal with the common elements Jim would face?

✓ His supervisor's direction?

Had his manager provided succinct influence on a daily basis to help Jim perform his job? Did it appear that his manager provided direction on how to prioritize tasks?

✓ Available resources?

Did Jim have the resources necessary to reach the performance objectives required of him? Were performance objectives clearly detailed by his manager?

Did his manager communicate deficiencies as well as strengths? Did his manager thrill in Jim's success or simply allow him to fail?

✓ Did Jim appear to be a motivated employee?

Was he a "keeper" in our company because he showed loyalty and a willingness to succeed? Was he trying his best?

My conclusions: Jim's motivation was NOT an issue, since he tried hard to do the right things. However, lacking the other fundamental tools, his motivation was inadequate to perform his duties.

Jim had too many balls in the air and he didn't have the capacity to juggle them unassisted. Failing to apply the correct order of importance, Jim had chugged along in a complacent state, feeling assured that he was meeting the company's expectations because he hadn't heard to the contrary from his superior. Jim's manager didn't assume responsibility for training, direction, influence, communications, supervision, and providing resources, and didn't evaluate Jim's experience to ensure he could perform the job. Expectations were lax—at best—and Jim also was carrying the weight of the manager's own deficiencies, and in the final analysis, we had failed *Jim*, not the other way around.

OK, as I pointed out earlier in the flight attendant position analysis and priority lists, how DOES one make accurate determinations regarding the priority assortment model and appropriate order of importance for tasks—especially a job that's as unstructured as that of a mid-level manager?

To begin with, broadly categorize the necessary functions, as I did when I described Jim's tasks. Then prioritize the categories and follow up with the individual tasks under that category. Those categories that are related can often share similar importance, such as Human Resource issues and Labor disputes, or Sales activity and revenue production.

THE most crucial functions for Jim would have been: Regulations, Safety, and Revenue/Expense control. Why? Because those areas had the most potential to negatively impact the organization's objectives. *Compliance activity* from a governmental agency can levy fines and even criminal indictments against the organization and its officers. *Safety* matters are self–explanatory—such as expenses, regulatory interaction, criminal and civil exposure, and moral issues. *Revenue/Expense control* is Business 101, so I don't need to say much about that.

Take a moment and prioritize the functions for Jim, based on what you've learned so far.

Charles N. Acker

Priorities for Jim

Training employees	Supervise two departments	Maintenance schedules	Regulatory compliance	Fleet utilization
Produce revenue	Control expenses	Prepare reports	Customer service	Vendor relationships
Human resources	Payroll	Capital issues	Sales	Policy enforcement
Hiring	Safety	Conferences	Communications	Labor disputes

Following is my selection:

1. Safety
2. Regulatory
3. Revenue accountability
4. Human resources
5. Customer service
6. Communications

I'd broaden the categories into those top six priorities and integrate other related functions into them, as follows:

Safety	Regulatory	Revenue	Human Resource	Customer Service	Communications
Training	Training	Sales	Hiring	Vendors	Reports
Maint.	Maint.	Expense	Labor	Supervision	Conferences
	Supervision	Fleet Util.	Payroll	Sales	
		Capital	Supervision		

Prioritize the new categories based on organizational impact. You'll note that several new groupings have the same functions. For example, Supervision crosses a wide spectrum and is applicable in several key areas, but the specific method of supervising would be applied to the key category. *HR* issues would cover employee contracts, pay, performance, and promotions, while *Regulatory* would cover policies, regulations, and compliance.

In the event that Jim was faced with multiple priorities, he could always base his activity on the order of one through six, the first being Safety-related matters. While that model won't cure all of the problems faced on the job, it does provide guidance for determining the most crucial issue to deal with. That's not to say that we won't have to deal with all the issues sooner or later, but perhaps we can delegate some of the other matters until we have the time to deal with them. If the company buys into AND participates in that assortment of priorities, we can be assured that we're following the performance objectives of the company. Now we just have to be certain to deal with the issues correctly and that's where a senior manager must assist in providing direction and influence.

As we did for the flight attendant, our model would read something like this:

1. **Safety**
2. **Regulatory** matters (closely associated with Safety)
3. **Revenue** (we first have to make certain that we stay in business)
4. **Human resources** (we must take care of our staff)
5. **Customer service** (we must take care of our customers)

6. **Communications** (we must analyze our position to ensure that we're on track with our objectives

(I'm not naïve. I understand that many companies place revenue as a first priority, but that's VERY dangerous, especially in the litigious corporate world of today. For example, how many companies can you think of that have fallen from grace because consumers believe that corporate profits were more important than safety? The list is endless. Consider Firestone Tire Company in the year 2000, for example. This is not to say that the company didn't consider safety as their number one priority—that's yet to be established as fact—but they've had a very difficult time proving it, and in the court of public opinion and law, PROVE it they must.)

You've heard me talk about the employee growth relationship, but what is it? It's made up of everything in this book. It's a conviction that dictates how we develop top performing employees who are loyal to our organization and mission. The conviction comes first from the company and then, only then, will our employees adopt it. A growth relationship is dictated by the principle that, as managers, our prime objective is to ensure that our employees grow beyond where they are today. That means selecting the right employee, training, supervision, resources, and motivating our staff to perform. It means recognizing improvement and building upon it for the future. It also means recognizing failures and developing educational tools and discipline to improve those deficiencies. It means a lot of things, but most importantly, it means to *thrill in success*.

You've also heard me talk about setting performance objectives, but how is that done? It's simple, really. Look at where you are, where you want to be, and what it will take to get there. Balance where you want to be with how to get there. Don't set objectives beyond what you're willing to spend to achieve them.

In conclusion. I want to leave you with some points to consider:

- ✓ Some employees choose to learn the hard way.
- ✓ You'll face "bad attitudes."
- ✓ Change is often painful.
- ✓ Thrill in success.
- ✓ The teacher is there for the student.
- ✓ Practice and preparation—remember the pit crew!
- ✓ Employee improvement is the manager's responsibility.
- ✓ Employees do what we inspect, not what we expect.
- ✓ Inspect when they don't expect it.
- ✓ Adopt the "smelly dog theory" if possible.
- ✓ Recruit the right employees by measuring their talent.
- ✓ Develop a position analysis.
- ✓ Keep employees informed about their progress.
- ✓ Clear up priority confusion.

- ✓ Don't ask employees to go beyond resource capacity.

- ✓ You get what you pay for.

- ✓ Manage different cultures differently.

- ✓ People will never rise above what we believe about them.

- ✓ Seek and give loyalty.

- ✓ Establish strategic plans—MAP your goals.

- ✓ Share your goals.

- ✓ Don't easily give up on employees.

- ✓ You may be training your replacement, but fear not—that means YOU can move up.

- ✓ The less of any one category you have, the more of another you must apply. Less talent, more training; less training, more supervision; less supervision, more motivation, and so on. We can eliminate natural talent if we have an abundance of everything else! Using these principles we find that the right dog CAN hunt.

Credit, References and Sources

- The Seattle Times

- *Snow White and the Seven Dwarves*, Walt Disney Productions

- *Waterdog* by Richard Wolters

- *Sherlock Holmes* by Sir Arthur Conan Doyle

- American Bus Association seminar: *Recruiting, Training and Hiring Employees*

- United Bus Association seminar: *Employee development for Top Performance*

- Gray Line Worldwide_convention seminars: *The Bear Trap, Developing a Powerful Workplace, American's with Disabilities Act, Changes in the Workplace, Recruiting and Hiring Top Drivers*

- Ontario Bus Association seminar: *That Dog Just Don't Hunt*

- Council on Hotel, Restaurant and Institutional Education: *Trends in the Hospitality Workforce.*

- Hundreds of employees and colleagues that continue to provide insights, direction and wonderful conversation.

Experience

- Regional Vice President, Transportation Management Services, Doha, Qatar

- Vice President Operations, Hotard Motorcoach Services

- Director Training and Safety, Holland America Line, Transportation Division

- Director Transportation, The Way International

- Past President, National Association of Fleet Supervisors

- Washington State Governors Safety Conference Committee Chair, transportation

- Seattle Community College District, Seattle, WA, Technical Advisory Board Member, Curriculum development

- Delgado Community College, New Orleans, LA, Hospitality curriculum advisor -

- Executive Committee, Bus Industry Safety Council

- Seymore Award, Best Service to Guests